Sewing Is Easy!

by **Helen Nicol Tanous**

photographs by **Henry John Tanous**

RANDOM HOUSE

NEW YORK

Contents

A bone needle is the sewing tool of Eskimos and other primitive people. For thousands of years they have used it to make beautiful clothes. But we find it is more convenient and a whole lot speedier to use a sewing machine. Ask your mother to show you how to run it. Then practice on paper in order to become really skillful.

Sew It Yourself

It's fun to sew. When you finish some useful article, you will feel a real thrill because you know that you made it with your own hands. Everyone wants to feel useful. For a girl it is especially important to become skilled in the home arts, for it will be her responsibility to make a happy home for others.

One of the most satisfying things a girl can learn to do is to make her own clothes. When you wear something that you have made yourself, you will glow with pride. Your friends will be filled with admiration for your ability and accomplishment. And it will please your parents to have you learn such a useful art.

You will also find that you save money by making your own clothes. More important, you will find it is more fun to wear things that are made for you alone.

The things that are shown in this book are all very easy to make. Anyone who will read carefully and follow directions exactly will soon become a competent seamstress. The experience you gain from making these things will help you go on to more complicated things. For successful sewing you need self-confidence, and this you will gain by learning the basic steps.

Sew it yourself and you will soon find that sewing is easy!

A congenial group of girls will find it fun to sew together.

Sewing With Your Friends

Sewing is a sociable hobby. Having company while you work adds to the fun you will get out of it. Try to find two or three friends who are interested in learning to sew. Perhaps you can form a sewing club which will meet regularly. In this way you will be able to exchange ideas which will be helpful to all of you. Probably you will accomplish more if you plan for weekly meetings. If all of you work on the same project, you will be able to help each other and compare your work.

Begin With a Plan

What do you want to make? What material will you use? When will you begin? These are the first questions you must be able to answer. When you have the answers, you have a plan. When you have a plan, you are ready to begin to sew. That sounds simple enough. But sometimes people sit down to sew before they have a plan. When that happens, they waste time and good materials. It is much better if they decide what to make, what material they will use, and when they will work.

As you plan to start sewing, be sure you have at least an hour for the first work period. Sewing will be easier if you have no interruptions.

The First Step
to Good Sewing

The first step to good sewing is to be neat. That means keeping your sewing tools in place, keeping your materials in order, and keeping your workroom neat. You will save time and energy if you learn to clean up as you go and to put your tools where they belong.

A good way to start is to get all your small supplies together in a box. A cigar box is ideal for this purpose. It will look very pretty, too, if you paint it or cover it with colored paper. In this box you should keep the following supplies:

a pair of shears
a small ruler
a tape measure
a box of pins
a package of needles
   (5 to 10 sharps are the best size)
safety pins
   (medium size and tiny gold ones)
elastic
   (½ inch wide and ¼ inch wide)
several spools of thread
a piece of chalk
a very soft pencil

A pair of good sharp shears is very important in good sewing. It is easier to work with a fairly large pair than with a small one even though your hands may be small. Be sure the shears are sharp; it is difficult to cut with dull ones. It will be nice if you can have a pair of your very own so that you can keep them in the box with your other supplies.

Now hunt up a large pretty box to hold material. Later you can use the same box to hold the article you are working on.

Sewing should always be a pleasant occupation and the more beauty you bring to it the pleasanter it is going to be. So be sure to keep all your small supplies in a small pretty box and your material and unfinished work in a large pretty box.

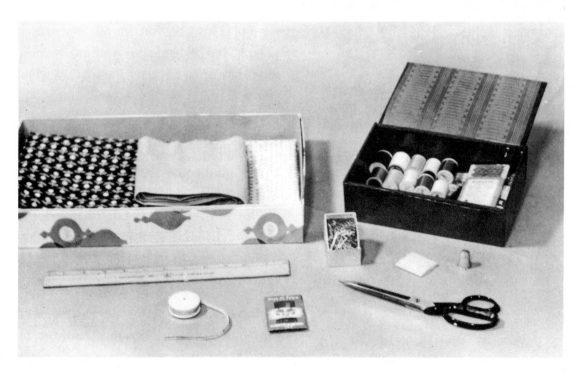

Sewing is much easier if you keep your tools in order and your materials neat.

Getting Ready to Sew

Sewing on your lap may cause all sorts of problems.

The best way to sew is to spread your work on a table.

Before you begin to sew, be sure that you are ready. See that your hair is brushed and your hands are clean. Be sure you have on a clean dress. Better still, wear a clean apron to protect the material you are working on. This may not sound like part of sewing, but it really is. Nothing is more important than to be neat and clean when you sew.

When you begin, be sure you have a good light. If you are right-handed, the light should come over your left shoulder. Then it will light up the work on which you are sewing. If you are left-handed, the light should come over your right shoulder. Daylight is better for sewing than artificial light.

The best way to sew is to sit at a table with your work neatly arranged in front of you. If you sit in a big comfortable chair with all your supplies in your lap, you may find that your skirt will be sewed right to whatever you are working on. And your supplies may easily slip down in the folds of your lap or the cracks of the chair.

How to Cut and Not to Cut

The right way to cut:
scissors won't cut the wood of the table.

The wrong way to cut:
they might cut the cover of the sofa.

One important part of sewing is cutting out the material. You will find that the best place to cut out your work is on a large bare table or on the floor. Then there will be no danger of your scissors cutting anything except the material which you want to cut.

If you try to cut on a bed or couch, you will almost certainly cut into something you had no intention of cutting, such as the bedspread or the couch cover.

When you lay out the material for cutting, be sure that there is nothing under it except the bare table or the floor!

Scissors and Shears

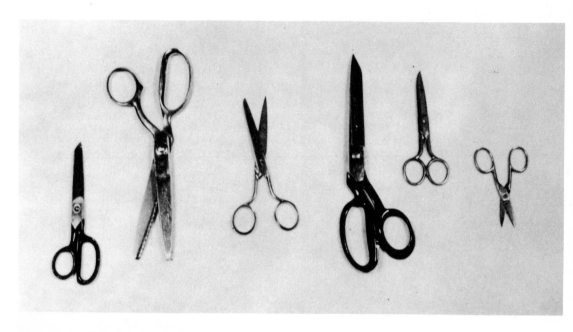

Scissors have two handles that are the same size.
Shears have one handle that is larger than the other.

A good seamstress knows the difference between scissors and shears and learns to use the right one at the right time.

To cut thread or small materials like ribbon and elastic, scissors do a good job. But to cut a piece of cloth, shears do a better job.

Scissors have two handles that are the same size. Shears have one handle that is larger than the other.

The large handle of a pair of shears is called the *bow* handle. When you cut with shears, put your thumb in the small handle, your pointing finger outside the bow handle to brace it, and the other fingers in the bow handle. You may find it is easier to put all four fingers inside the bow handle.

It is easier to cut with shears because you are able to use the muscles of your whole hand and arm. When you cut with shears, your hand and fingers will not get tired so easily.

When you cut with scissors, put your thumb through one handle and one finger through the other. Cutting will be easier if you put your second finger through the handle and brace the outside of the handle with your pointing finger.

Whether you use shears or scissors, be sure that the narrow, pointed blade slides under the cloth.

When you cut with scissors, put your thumb through one handle and one finger through the other.

When you cut with shears, put your thumb through the small handle and three fingers through the bow handle.

Shapes to Know

In making patterns you will need to become familiar with the shapes shown on this page and with the names for them.

Square

SQUARE   A shape like this with all four sides the same length.

CIRCLE   Round, like this.

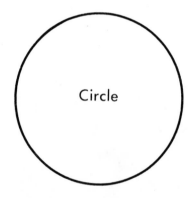

Circle

Rectangle

RECTANGLE   A shape like this with two sides that are longer than the other two sides.

TRIANGLE   A shape like this with three points.

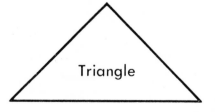

Triangle

Learning to Measure

You also have to know how to measure correctly. Learn what the markings mean on your ruler and tape measure.

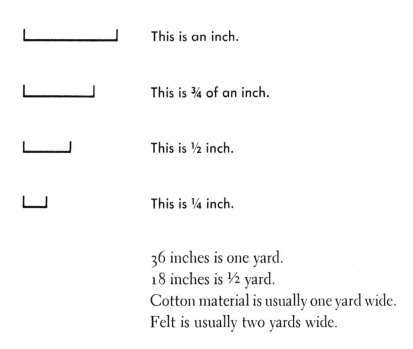

This is an inch.

This is ¾ of an inch.

This is ½ inch.

This is ¼ inch.

36 inches is one yard.
18 inches is ½ yard.
Cotton material is usually one yard wide.
Felt is usually two yards wide.

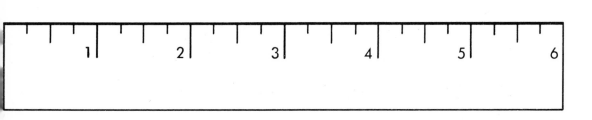

This is a six-inch ruler. When you measure, be sure to start from the very edge. From the edge of the ruler to the first long mark is one inch.

Warp and Woof

As you know, cloth is made from threads that are woven together. Knowing how these threads are put together will help you recognize which is *lengthwise* and which is *crosswise* of the material. This is important in planning and cutting your patterns.

In weaving, the first threads that are laid on the loom go lengthwise. They are called the *warp*. The warp is the lengthwise grain. These threads are usually stronger and are pulled tighter than the crosswise threads. They are pulled tight in order to support the weight of the crosswise threads. Because they are pulled tight, they will shrink more in washing than the crosswise threads.

The crosswise threads that are woven under and over from edge to edge are called the *woof* or *filling* threads. These threads are not pulled so tight as the lengthwise threads. Because of this, the material will be more likely to stretch on the crosswise grain.

At each edge the woof thread is turned back to cross the warp again. The loops made by turning the thread at the edges are called the selvedge which means "self-edge." The selvedge always runs along the length of the cloth.

Find a small scrap of cloth and see if you can tell which is the warp and which is the woof. Hold the scrap up to the light or look at it under a magnifying glass. The warp threads will be a little straighter and coarser than the woof threads. The woof threads are softer and more wiggly. Pull out a few threads from each direction and see which ones break more easily.

Examine a scrap of cloth under a magnifying glass
and see if you can tell the warp from the woof.

It is important to know what is meant by a lengthwise fold and a crosswise fold of material.

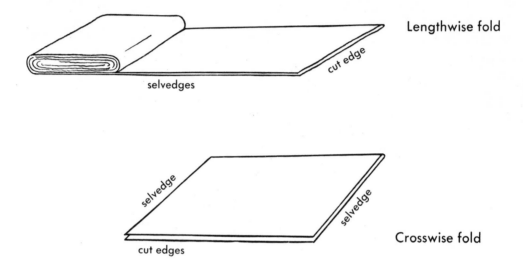

Lengthwise fold

cut edge

selvedges

Crosswise fold

selvedge

selvedge

cut edges

If you pull the cloth this way, you will be able to straighten it.

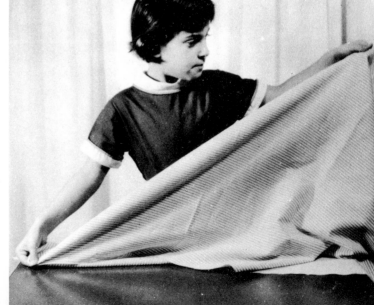

18

Straightening the Cloth

Sometimes you may find it necessary to straighten a piece of cloth before you can cut anything out of it.

If your cloth, when folded lengthwise, is even at the top and the bottom then it does *not* need to be straightened. Diagram 1, at the right, shows cloth that is even and does not need straightening.

If your cloth, when folded lengthwise, is *uneven* at the top and the bottom, then it does need to be straightened. Diagram 2 shows a piece of cloth that is *uneven* and *does* need to be straightened.

Unfold the cloth that needs straightening. It will look like Diagram 3. Take hold of corner A with one hand, and hold corner B with the other hand. Stretch the cloth until it is even. You may have to stretch several times. Do it until the cloth lies even when folded lengthwise.

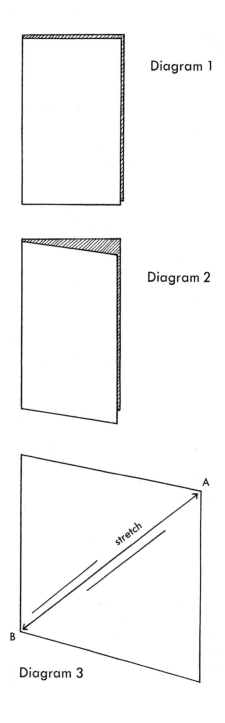

Diagram 1

Diagram 2

Diagram 3

Needles and Thread

Kinds of needles

darner

crewel

sharp

between

Needle sizes

3
4
5
6
7
8
9
10

There are many different kinds of needles, and most of them come in many different sizes. The four kinds of needles that you will be most apt to find in the store are darners, crewels, sharps and betweens.

A darner is a large, long needle with an eye large enough for yarn.

A crewel needle, which is another name for an embroidery needle, is a short needle with a long eye. It is easier to thread than a sharp.

A sharp is short and has a small eye.

A between is short and slimmer at the eye-end than a sharp. It is even harder to thread because the eye is smaller.

For ordinary sewing, choose either a sharp or a crewel, whichever you find easier to thread. The best size to use is a number 7. Needle sizes run from 3 to 10; the smaller the number the larger the needle.

You can buy needles in packets all of one size or in assorted sizes. An assorted packet of 3 to 9 or of 5 to 10 is a good choice.

When you thread a needle, brace one hand against the other. This will help you to keep the needle steady.

After your needle is threaded, measure the thread from your extended hand to your shoulder. This is the right length for you.

Tying a Knot

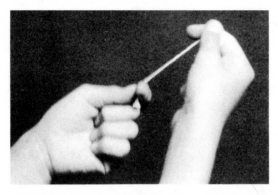

1. Hold the end of the thread with your left hand.

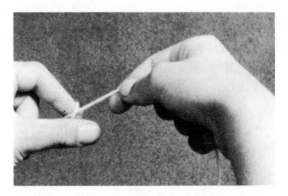

2. Wrap the thread once around your fore-finger.

3. Roll the loop forward with your thumb.

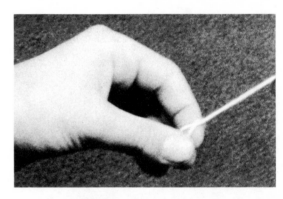

4. Pull your forefinger out of the loop.

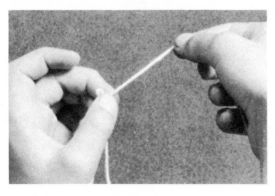

5. With your middle finger tighten the loop.

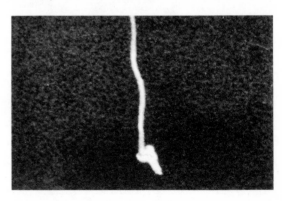

6. Your finished knot should look like this.

Sewing With a Thimble

In order to get a needle through a piece of cloth, you have to give it a push from the back. But a needle is almost as sharp in the rear as it is in the front. So you need a thimble to protect your pushing finger.

You can get a thimble at the ten-cent store. To get the right size, keep trying them on in the store until you find one that just fits the middle finger of your right hand. If you are left-handed, fit the middle finger of your left hand.

At first you may find it a little awkward to wear a thimble. But roller skates were awkward the first time you put them on, too. After you use a thimble for a little while, you will find that it helps you sew quickly and easily. You will never want to sew without one.

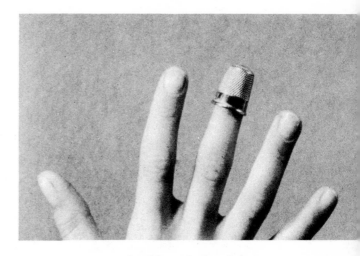

After you use a thimble a little while, you will never sew without one.

Hand Stitching

There are four basic stitches in hand sewing that you should learn right away.

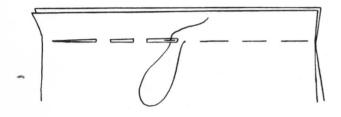

Basting Stitch: This is a long running stitch that is meant to be temporary. That is, it is used to hold two pieces of material together until you are ready to machine stitch them. In basting you should use two lengths of stitches, first a long stitch and then a short one. The long stitches are made on top and the short ones underneath. You can take several stitches before pulling the thread through the material.

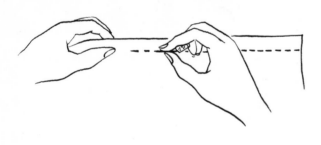

Running Stitch: This should be a row of evenly spaced stitches all the same length. They should be rather short, not more than ¼ inch long.

The running stitch is used to hold together two pieces of material which will have very little pull or strain.

Back Stitch: This stitch is made by sewing one stitch forward then one backward. After you take one stitch forward, you go back to the end of the last stitch and start the next stitch there. Thus you come out with a solid line of stitching which of course is very strong.

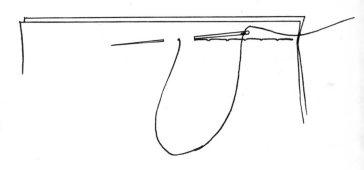

Blind Stitch: The blind stitch is used mostly for finishing hems, where you do not want the stitches to show from the right side. Take a very small stitch catching two or three threads of fabric at the edge of the folded hem. Slide the point of the needle along under the fold for about ⅛ inch and bring the needle up through the fold. Repeat. The stitches should be straight, small and hardly visible.

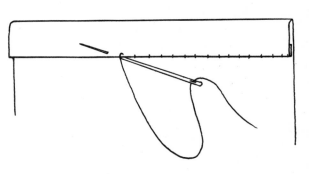

Machine Stitching

Learning to run a sewing machine with skill requires practice just as learning to dance or play the piano takes practice.

First of all, have someone who is experienced teach you how to operate the machine. You will need to know how to thread it, how to start and how to stop it.

Then, before you begin sewing on cloth, you should practice stitching on folded paper with an unthreaded needle. Wrapping paper is fine for this. Draw lines on the paper, as shown in the diagrams. Even though the needle is not threaded, the presser foot must be down to sew. This holds the material or paper in place. Stitch along the lines as closely as you can, guiding the paper with your hands. Never pull the paper faster than it wants to go. Hold it very lightly so that you guide without pulling.

You will be able to tell from the perforations in the paper just how skillful you were in guiding the machine. Practice with several sheets until you can stitch a perfectly straight line and can turn corners and curves easily.

Learning to control the speed of the machine is just as important as learning to sew straight. So practice that too. Learn to increase and decrease your speed smoothly. Remember that you are trying to learn to control the machine. Don't let it control you!

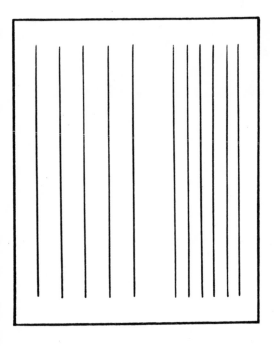

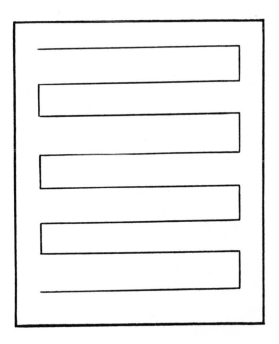

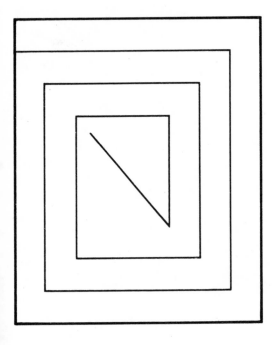

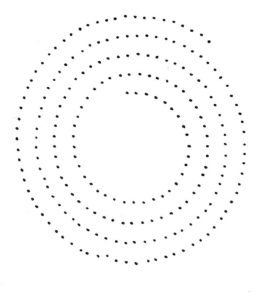

Dishtowel Apron

Materials You Will Need

1 hemmed dishtowel
1 card of at least eight plastic rings
1½ yards of ribbon, one inch wide
Thread to match the main color of the
    towel

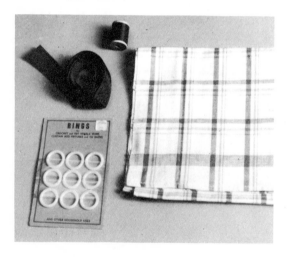

These are the supplies you will need.

Fold in eight pleats at the top.

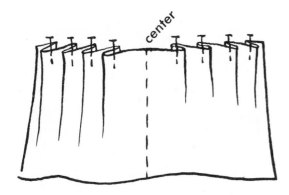

Fold the towel in half and put a pin in one edge to mark the center. Now make four folds or pleats on each side of the center of the towel. Take up about 2 inches in each fold. Fold the material toward the sides, away from the center. Be sure that the last fold is near the edge. Hold each fold in place with a pin.

At each fold or pleat, sew one of the plastic rings. Have your thread double and sew each ring in place with enough stitches to make it secure. When you have the rings in place, thread the ribbon through the plastic rings and your apron is all finished.

When the apron goes to the laundry, you had better take out the ribbon because it might fade onto the cloth.

Sew a ring at each fold.

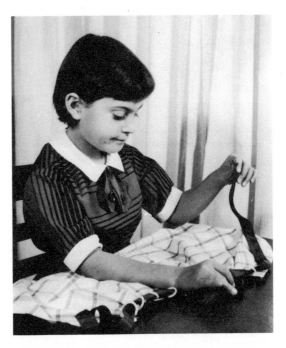

Thread the ribbon through the rings.

Fringed Table Mats

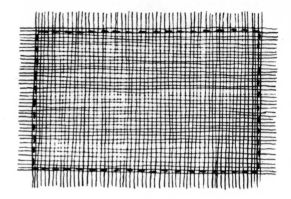

Materials You Will Need

One yard of 36-inch material
Thread to match

Fringed table mats are a quick and easy sewing project. And almost anybody's mother or aunt is delighted to receive six table mats for a gift.

The first step is to select the material you will use. Because you will fringe the material, it is important to get cloth with a fairly coarse weave. Monk's cloth and Indianhead are good washable fabrics that fringe easily.

By following the pattern below, you can get six table mats out of one yard of 36-inch material.

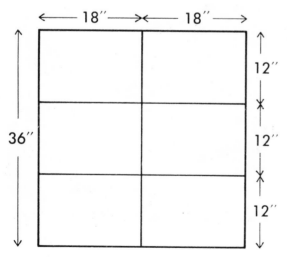

But before you begin to cut, you will need to get your material ready. First draw a thread at each cut end to be sure the material is straight. Cut along the line of the thread. Next, trim off the selvedge edges. Now, measure twelve inches from one end and draw a thread as a guide to cutting. With a pin, pull one thread of the material at the 12-inch mark. Gently pull it all the way across the goods. If the thread breaks, use the pin again to pull out the end of the same thread and continue until one entire crosswise thread is pulled out.

Using this line as a guide, cut the 12-inch strip from the larger piece of material. Measure off another 12-inch strip, draw the thread as before, and cut it off from the rest. Now you have three strips of material 36 inches wide and 12 inches deep.

Fold each strip in two so that each half will be just 18 inches wide. Draw a lengthwise thread and cut the strip in two pieces. Each will measure 12 inches by 18 inches, the size for one table mat.

Now you are ready to fringe the four sides of each table mat. Keep pulling threads from the edge until you have ½ inch of fringe on each side. Be sure that you pull the threads gently so that they will not break or become tangled.

When you have finished pulling threads, make a line of machine stitching just inside the fringe. On the diagram the stitching is shown by a dotted line. This stitching will help to hold the fringe in place and will prevent raveling when the finished mats are washed.

In the same way, you can make napkins to match the table mats if you wish. A good size for napkins is 12 inches square. That means you can get six napkins out of ⅔ yard of 36-inch material.

Tray covers, dresser scarfs, card-table covers, and dolls' bedspreads can be made in much the same manner. Just be sure that you measure carefully before you begin to draw threads. This can't be a guessing game. The yardstick or tape measure will help you more than the best guesses in the world.

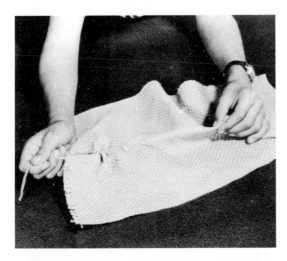

Pull a thread to give yourself a straight line for cutting.

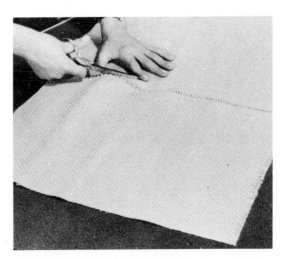

Cut carefully on the line you made by pulling the thread.

Plastic Envelope for Table Mats

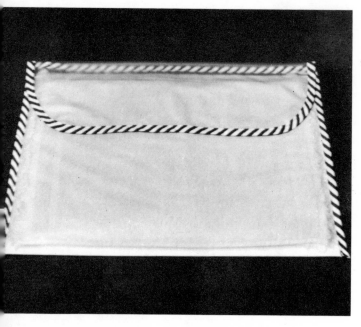

Materials You Will Need

⅝ yard of clear plastic
1 package of wide bias binding
Thread to match the binding
Piece of cardboard at least 12 by 18
    inches

A plastic envelope for table mats is a very welcome gift and a very easy and inexpensive one to make. The plastic material costs only 25 or 35 cents a yard and is 54 inches wide. The cardboard can be cut from the top or bottom of an old suit box. The cardboard is used to stiffen the envelope so that the mats will not flop around and get wrinkled.

To Cut the Material

Cut the plastic into a rectangle (with nice square corners) 32 inches long and 19 inches wide. Save the large piece that is left to make into something else later. Cut the cardboard into a rectangle 12 inches wide and 18 inches long. The cardboard is a little smaller so that it will be easy to slip into the envelope.

To Sew the Envelope

First baste and then stitch a piece of bias binding onto one of the short ends of the plastic. Round the corners of the other short end. Round corners are easier to bind than square corners.

Fold the plastic into an envelope that measures 13 by 19 inches with a 6-inch flap.

Now you are ready to baste binding around the envelope. Start at corner A and continue on around to corner B. Be sure that you catch both thicknesses of the plastic into the binding. At both corners, fold the raw edges of the binding under so it will look very neat. Stitch it on the machine and remove the bastings. Last of all slip the cardboard into place.

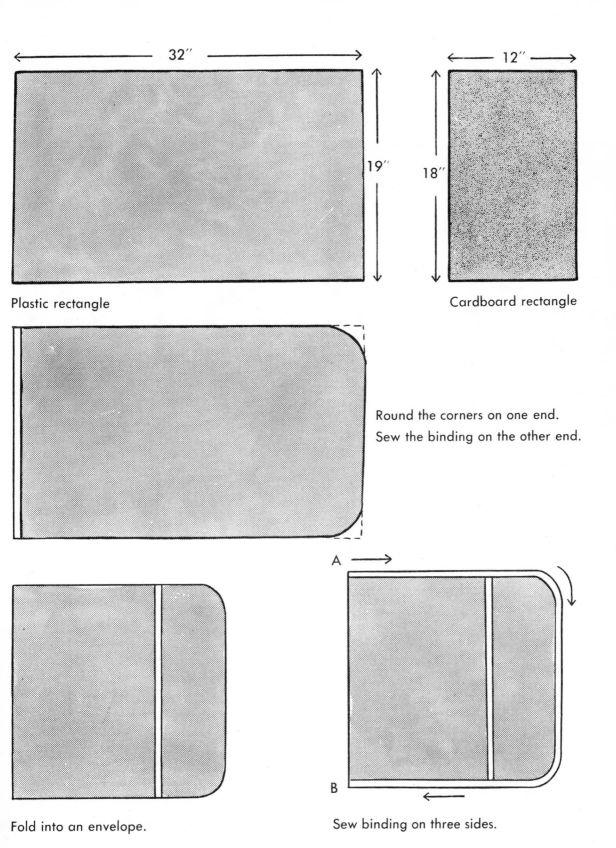

32″

19″

Plastic rectangle

12″

18″

Cardboard rectangle

Round the corners on one end.
Sew the binding on the other end.

Fold into an envelope.

A

B

Sew binding on three sides.

Pot Holders, Plain and Fancy

Materials You Will Need

8-inch squares of gay material

8-inch squares of cotton batting, cotton quilting, or heavy woolen material for lining

Wide bias binding available in any ten-cent store

Thread to match the tape

Pot holders are very easy to make and your mother will probably be delighted to have some new ones. They don't take much material or much work, but they will give you a lot of experience in cutting and sewing. They can be made from left-over scraps of material.

Let's begin with a simple square pattern. For this you will need two squares of material for the outside of the pot holder and another 8-inch square of the heavy cotton batting or quilting for the lining.

Put the lining between the two pieces of outside material. Baste these together around the edge as in Diagram A. Baste the bias binding around the edge so that it covers the raw edges of the material. Now machine stitch the binding and pull out the basting threads. You will also have to machine stitch the pot holder several times to keep the lining in place. Sew from corner to corner and then straight across as shown in Diagram B. In one corner sew a plastic ring so that the pot holder can be hung up to await a hurry call for duty in the kitchen.

Below are patterns for the two fancy pot holders shown in the photo. Diagram C is the pattern for the tulip, and Diagram D is the pattern for the four-petaled flower.

Take a piece of paper 8 inches square; fold it in half. Mark the paper into 1 inch squares just like the diagram. Draw in the pattern you want. Be sure to have the edge marked "fold" laid on the fold of the paper. Cut out the pattern, open it up and pin it onto your cloth. Draw around the pattern with a crayon or soft pencil. Cut out the holder and make it just as you did the square one.

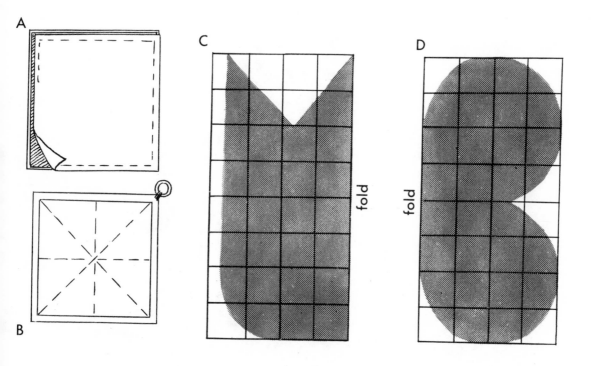

Barbecue Mitts

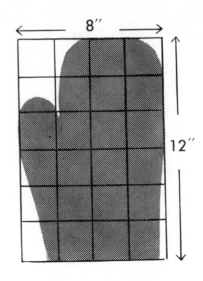

8"

12"

Materials You Will Need

½ yard of reversible cotton quilting

1 package of wide bias binding in a contrasting color

1 spool of thread to match the binding

To Make Your Pattern

Cut a piece of paper which is 8 inches wide and 12 inches long. Mark it off in 2-inch squares as in the diagram at the left. Then draw the outline of a mitt on the paper. Cut out the pattern of the mitt. It will be shaped like the shaded part of the diagram.

To Cut Out the Material

Fold the material in half with the fold going across. Lay your pattern at one end, and draw around it three times just as the boy in the picture is doing. When the patterns are all marked, cut around each one. In each case, be sure to cut through the double thickness of quilting. This will give you six pieces of material the shape of a mitt.

To Sew the Material

Make two stacks of mitts with three pieces of material in each stack. If your material is different on the two sides, then decide which is to be the *wrong* side. Lay each stack of mitts with the wrong side outside. Have them face each other as in the diagram at the right.

Put a pin through the top layer of material in each stack. Leave these pins in place until you have finished.

Next, pin the edges of each stack of material to hold them together until you can sew them. Place the pins as they are in the diagram. Machine stitch each mitt all around except at the bottom. That is the wrist opening. Remove the pins from the edge.

Now baste the bias binding around the wrist opening of each mitt. Be sure that both edges of bias binding are caught with your basting stitches. Machine stitch the binding as close to the edge as you can. Remove the basting threads. Turn the mitts right side out so that the seams are on the inside.

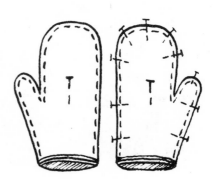

Workshop Apron

Materials You Will Need

- 1 yard of denim or striped ticking (for grown-up size) or ⅔ yard of denim or striped ticking (for junior size)
- 1 package of ½-inch white twill tape
- 1 spool of white thread, size 50 or coarser

Deep tone denim or striped ticking makes a nice sturdy apron to use in the workshop or in barbecue cooking. Made in the grown-up size it will be a nice gift for the man of the house. And in the junior size it will be just right for young cooks, carpenters and painters.

To Cut Out the Material

An apron is so simple that you will not even need to cut a pattern. Fold your material lengthwise and smooth it out so that the selvedges are together. With a soft pencil draw in the shape as it is shown in this diagram for the grown-up size. Cut out the part which is shaded on the diagram. Cut two pockets from the scrap pieces so that each one is 7½ by 8 inches. The 7½-inch side should be on the selvedge.

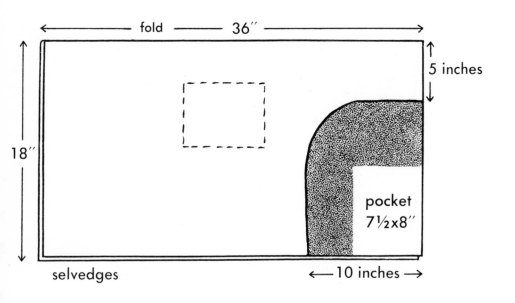

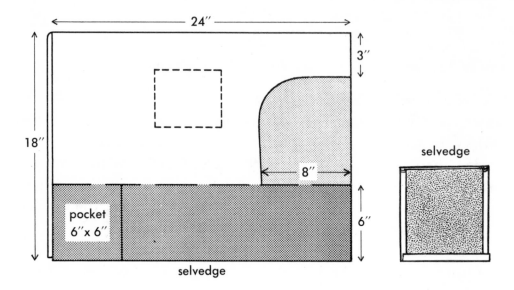

The material will be too wide for the junior size apron so the first thing to do is to cut off a piece from the selvedge sides. Cut off a 6-inch strip from each side. Then cut out your apron using the measurements given in the diagram here.

The strip to be cut off is shown with dark shading on the diagram. Cut the pockets out of this left-over piece. Make the pocket 6 inches square and have one edge laid on the selvedge. The selvedge will be the top of the pocket and will not need hemming as the selvedge itself is a nice finish.

Turn down ½ inch on the other three sides of each pocket. Crease it with your fingers so that it stays turned under. Pin the pockets onto the apron as shown by the dotted line on the diagram. Stitch them down carefully keeping near the edge. Make nice square corners.

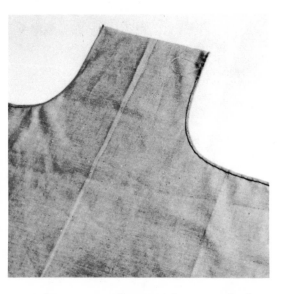

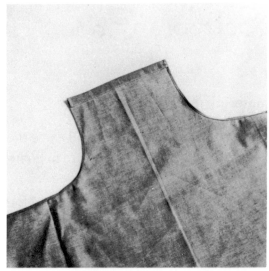

Make a narrow hem on the curved edges of the apron. On the junior apron also make a narrow hem down each side. Baste these narrow hems and machine stitch.

Turn down a ¾-inch hem at the top of the bib. Turn the raw edge under so that there is a clean edge to the hem. Baste in place, and then machine stitch.

Turn up 1½ inches at the bottom of the apron. Turn the raw edge under. Pin or baste the hem in place, and then machine stitch.

Sew on the tapes as shown here. Stitch them several times so that they will not pull off. Remove all basting threads, and press your apron.

Scissors Case

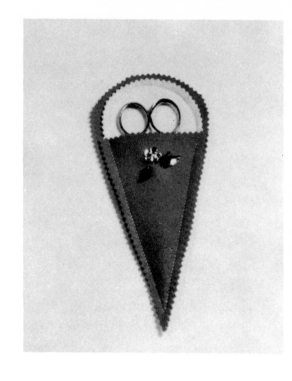

Materials You Will Need

A large piece of felt more than twice the
size of the scissors which are to go into the case

One smaller piece of felt in a contrasting
color

Thread to match one or the other kind
of felt

Making a pretty case for your sewing
shears or scissors will help you to remember
always to put them away carefully. Or it
will make a lovely gift for someone in your
family.

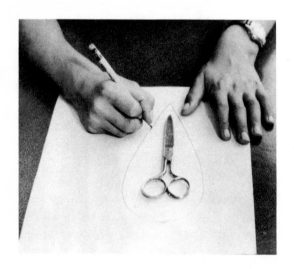

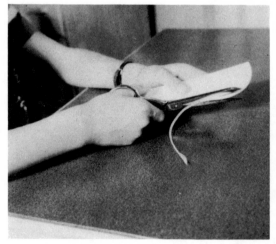

Lay the scissors or shears on a piece of
paper. Draw around them, keeping the line
about ½ inch from the point and handles.

Cut the pattern out and then fold it in
half lengthwise. Now trim the edges so
that both sides match.

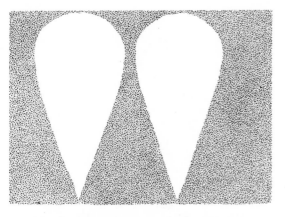

1. Place this pattern on a sheet of paper and cut another piece just like the first.

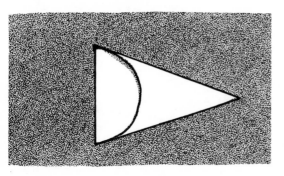

2. Fold one paper pattern down about two inches from the top edge and cut off the rounded top.

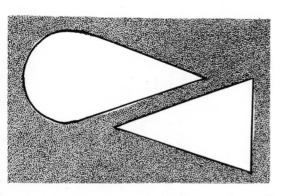

3. Lay both patterns on the larger piece of felt. With a pencil trace around them. Then cut on the pencil lines. Cut with pinking shears if you have them.

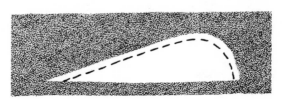

4. Now fold the larger pattern in half lengthwise. Trim off ¼ inch as shown with the dotted line above. Now place this smaller pattern on the contrasting felt and cut it out. Use pinking shears if you have them.

5. Lay all three pieces of felt together so that the contrasting color is in the middle. Pin the three together at the edges. Machine stitch all around as shown by the dotted line in the diagram.

6. Decorate the top piece with felt flowers or imitation jewels.

Doll Hat

Materials You Will Need

Piece of felt 7 inches square
¾ yard fringe or rickrack
¾ yard ribbon

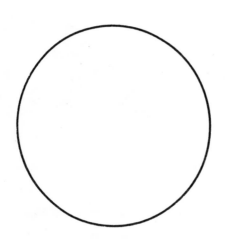

To Cut the Hat

1. This hat is so easy to make that you don't need a pattern at all. Just place a saucer or butter plate upside down on the felt. Draw around it with a crayon or soft pencil. Cut it out.

To Make the Hat

2. Baste the fringe around the outside edge of the felt circle. Now machine stitch or back stitch by hand to hold the fringe on securely.

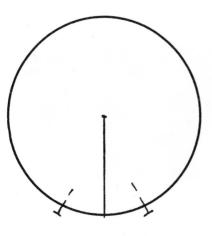

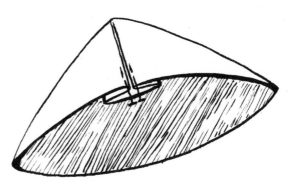

3. Make a pencil mark in the center of the circle; draw a straight line from that mark to the outside edge. Measure 2 inches away from the line on the outside edge of the circle. Place a pin there. Now measure 2 inches away from the other side of the line still on the outside edge of the circle. Put another pin there.

4. Fold the hat so that the two pins meet each other right on the straight line. Pin the two folds in place. Now your circle will look like a shallow cone or a coolie hat.

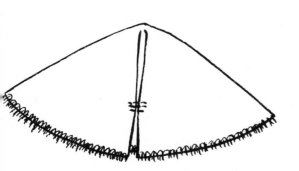

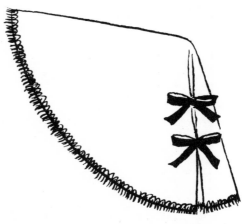

5. Sew the fold together about halfway between the outside edge and the center of the hat.

6. Make two bows from the ribbon. Sew one bow right over your stitches which are holding the fold together. Sew the other bow to the hat 1 inch above the first bow.

Felt Envelope Purse

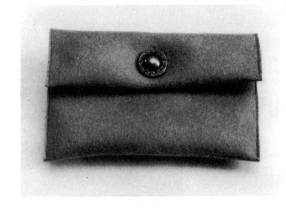

Materials You Will Need

¼ yard of felt
Spool of thread to match
1 large button
Box of fake jewels (if you want to decorate the purse)

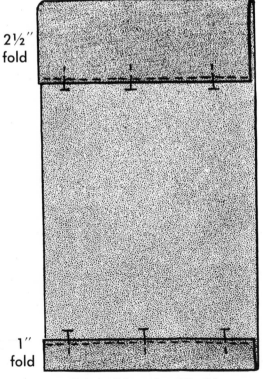

2½″ fold

1″ fold

felt 16″ long by 8″ wide

Cut a piece of felt 16 inches long and 8 inches wide. Fold one end down one inch. Hold it in place with three or four pins as in the diagram. Next, fold the other end down 2½ inches. Put in a few pins to hold it in place. Now stitch these two hems on the sewing machine. The stitching is shown on the diagram with dotted lines. The deep hem will be the flap of your purse.

Now fold the narrow hem up to meet the deep hem as shown in the diagram. The folded edge of the narrow hem should just meet the cut edge of the wide hem. Pin the sides together to make the sides of the purse. Stitch both sides on the sewing machine.

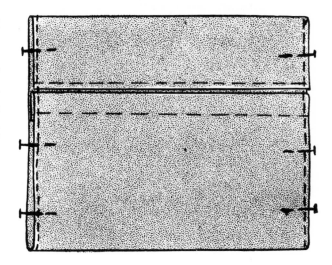

Now you will need a button and a buttonhole to keep your purse fastened. Find a pretty button that measures about ¾ of an inch across. Sew it to the center of the lower part of the purse. Have the thread double for added strength and be sure to start with the knot inside where it won't show.

Cut a slash in the flap for the buttonhole. It should be the same length as the button. Now sew loosely over the edges around the buttonhole.

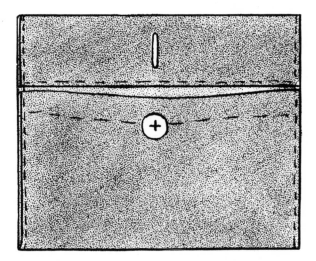

If you want a very fancy purse, you may want to decorate it with fake jewels which you can buy by the box in the ten-cent store.

Pony-Tail Hat and Scarf

Materials You Will Need

½ yard of tubular jersey
1 spool of thread to match the jersey
A plastic headband

Wool jersey is a very good material to use for this hat and scarf set because it can be fringed merely by cutting the edges. The fringe will remain neat because jersey does not fray. Since jersey is a stretchy material, one size hat will fit anyone.

Jersey is made in many beautiful plain colors and in a wide variety of stripes and patterns. It will be easy for you to find just the right material to look pretty with your winter coat or with warm play clothes.

Probably you can buy the plastic headband at the same store that sells the jersey. If not, you will find one in almost any variety store. Such a headband usually costs ten or fifteen cents. You need this headband to give shape and stiffness to the front edge of your pony-tail hat.

49

To Cut a Pattern

Cut a piece of paper 12 inches wide and 18 inches long. Mark it off into 2-inch squares. There will be six 2-inch squares on the short side and nine 2-inch squares on the long side.

Now draw the shape of the hat as shown in the diagram below. Cut off the part that is shaded on the diagram.

To Cut the Material

The hat: Place the pattern on the cloth so that the 14-inch side is on a fold and the 11-inch side is on the cut edge. Pin the pat-tern in place. Now cut around the curved edge. Clip the fringe as shown. The cuts should be about ½ inch apart and 2 inches deep. They will have to be a little wider apart at the bottom since the inside curve is smaller than the outside curve. Be sure to leave the unfringed section as shown on the diagram. This is where you will seam the hat together. The seam is shown by a dotted line.

The cord for the hat: Follow the directions in the diagram. Note that the short end is on a fold. This will give you a strip 24 inches long and 1½ inches wide.

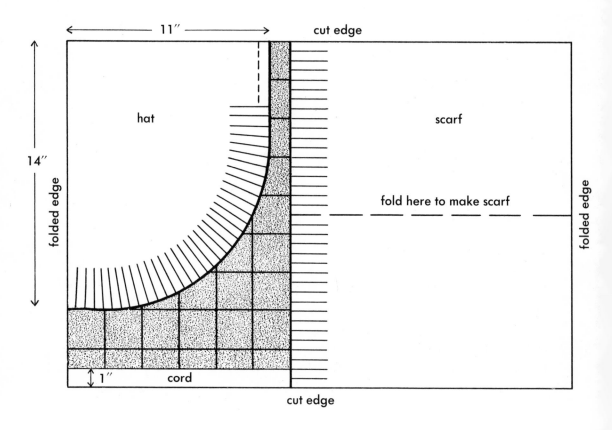

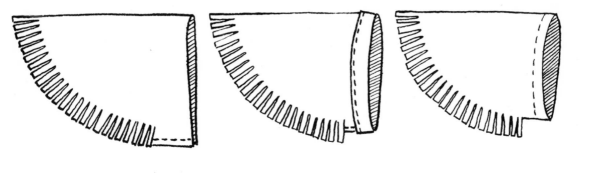

To Sew the Material

The hat: Fold the material so that the wrong side is outside. Pin the seam edges together. Machine stitch or back stitch ½ inch from the edges. Remove the pins. Fold back 1 inch for the casing and pin in place. Hand stitch it down except in one small spot in the back. Remove pins. Turn the hat inside out. Now the seam and hem will be on the inside. Slip your plastic headband into the front of the casing.

The cord for the hat: Pull the narrow strip until the cut edges curl inward. Leave the cut edges curled in. Then with tiny hand stitches catch the top edges where they begin to curl under. Make the stitches as nearly invisible as possible. Tie a knot in each end of the cord.

Put the hat on your head and have someone pull the fringed edges up into a pony tail. Tie the cord in a bow around the "pony tail" to hold it in place.

The scarf: Cut a scarf out of the left-over piece of jersey as shown in the diagram. Refold it so that the wrong side is on the outside. Have the fold go across so that the folded piece is 30 inches long and 9 inches from the folded edge to the cut edges. Pin the long cut edges together and baste. Remove the pins. Then machine stitch or back stitch along the row of bastings. Pull out the basting threads and turn the scarf so that the cut edges of the seam are on the inside. Fringe both ends to match the hat.

Gathered Skirt

Materials You Will Need

- 2 yards of cotton material 36 inches wide
- A spool of thread to match
- A button or hooks and eyes for the closing

After you have learned to sew by hand and on the machine and have practiced your new skill, you will be ready to make a gathered skirt for yourself.

In order to make a skirt, you must know your waist measure and the length of your skirts. Take the measurement of your waist with a tape measure. Pull the tape just tight enough to be comfortable. To this measurement add 2 inches. This extra amount is for the seam and overlap. On a slip of paper write down your total waist measure (that is, your waist measure plus 2 inches).

To find your skirt length, measure one of your skirts which fits you correctly. Measure it from the waistline seam (where the band is attached to the skirt) to the bottom of the hem. To this measurement add 4 inches. The extra 4 inches allows for the hem and for the waistline seam. Write this total skirt measurement on the same slip of paper as your waist measure. Keep these measurements with your sewing supplies.

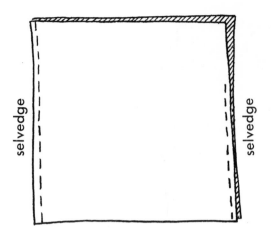

To Cut the Material

You will not need a pattern for the skirt. But you will have to measure carefully before you cut.

First, be sure to straighten your material if it needs it. (See page 18 for directions on straightening cloth.) Now lay the folded material out on your cutting table. Measure off your total skirt length (the length of your skirt plus 4 inches for hem and seam). Cut two pieces this same length.

Measure and cut two pieces of material for the skirt.

Cut a waistband and placket strip from the leftover material.

From the remaining material cut a piece of material for the waistband. This should be 4 inches wide and as long as your total waist measure.

Next, cut a strip of material which is 14 inches long and 3 inches wide. This is for the placket of your skirt.

To Sew the Skirt

Spread the two skirt lengths on top of each other on your cutting table. The two right sides should be inside facing each other. The selvedges should be together on each side.

Pin the selvedges together on each side so you will have ½-inch seams. Machine stitch or back stitch one side from top to bottom. On the other side stitch all but seven inches at the top. This opening will be for the placket of your skirt. Remove the pins.

Now you must gather the top edge of the skirt—the edge where you left the opening for the placket. To do this, use double thread and make a running stitch. The stitches should be rather small so that the material will gather evenly. You must run the gathering stitches from one side of the opening around the top of the skirt to the other side of the opening. Now pull on the gathering thread until the top of the gathered skirt measures the same as your waist measurement.

Pin the selvedges together before sewing the side seams.

Gather the top edge so that it will fit your waist.

Making a Placket

Step 1: Place the RIGHT side of the placket strip against the RIGHT side of the skirt. Have the side opened up as straight as possible. Baste the strip to the opening from one top edge to the other. Machine stitch the placket strip in place.

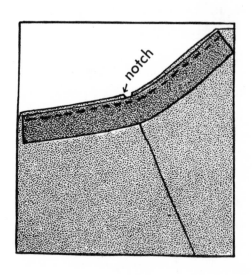

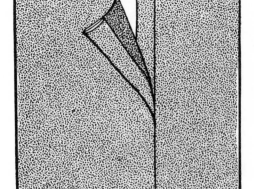

Step 2: Fold the strip in half with the fold turning to the inside of the skirt. Fold the raw edge under and hand stitch as shown.

Wrong side

front   back

Step 3: Have the placket extend out on the back side of the skirt. Fold it under on the front and tack in place at the top.

Right side

To Sew on the Waistband

Step 1: Fold the waistband lengthwise so that the right side of the material is on the inside. Stitch the two ends. Turn so that the raw edges are inside and the right side of the material is then outside. Press the long fold of the waistband.

Step 2: Place the waistband on the outside of the skirt so that the raw edges of the waistband are even with the raw edges of the skirt as in the first picture. Pin the gathered skirt to the inside of the waistband. Be sure that the placket is folded under on the front and extended on the back. Machine stitch the waistband in place making a seam ½ inch wide. Remove the pins.

Step 3: Fold the waistband over to the inside of the skirt. Turn under ½ inch at the raw edge of the band. Pin the band in place all the way around the waist being sure that you cover up the waistline seam. Place the pins every two or three inches. Now you are ready to hand stitch the band with very small, neat stitches. Remove the pins as you come to them.

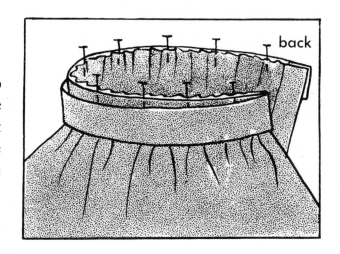

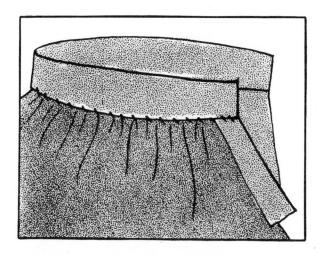

To Hem the Skirt

Turn up ½ inch of the skirt on the wrong side. Machine stitch this fold. Using a ruler to measure, put a row of pins on the inside of the skirt 3 inches from the bottom. Using this row of pins as a guide, turn up the hem. Pin all the way around. Hand stitch the hem in place with small stitches. Try to make the stitches invisible from the right side. Remove all pins.

Ruffled Blouse

Materials You Will Need

1¼ yards of 36-inch cotton material
1 package white bias binding
Thread to match the blouse material
White thread for the binding

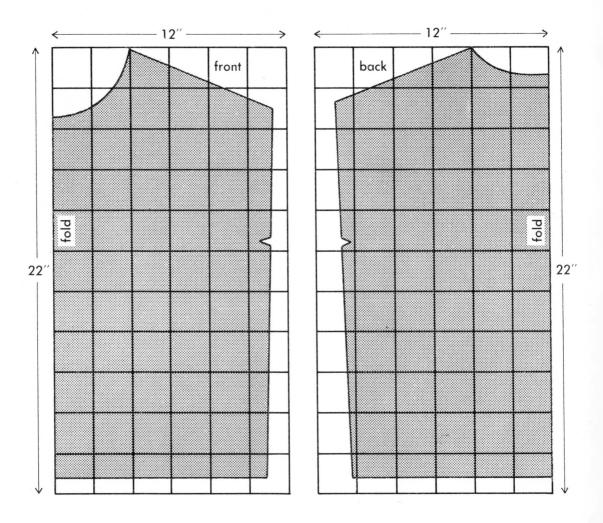

the notch at the side as it is on the diagram. The notch is there to tell you how large an opening to leave for your arm. After you have made the front pattern, copy the back pattern in the same way.

To Cut the Material

Fold your material in half lengthwise. Lay it on a bare table or on the floor. Lay your patterns on the material with the side marked "fold" on the fold of the material. Pin the patterns to the material and cut around them. From the left-over piece of material cut a long strip for the ruffle. The ruffle should measure 2½ inches wide and as long as the entire piece of material (1¼ yards long). When you cut the strip for the ruffle be sure that you have the selvedge for one of the long sides.

To Make the Pattern

Take a large sheet of paper at least 12 inches wide by 22 inches long. Mark it off into two-inch squares and then draw in the front pattern as it is on the large diagram. Be sure to write the word "fold" on your pattern in the same place that it is on the diagram. You must also be sure to make

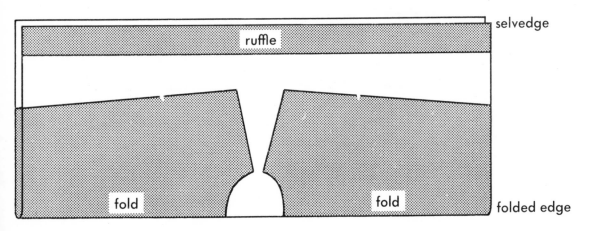

To Sew the Blouse

In making the blouse you will learn how to make a French seam. This is a nice way to finish lightweight material, for a French seam does not have any raw edges left to ravel. To make a French seam you first sew the two pieces of material together with the raw edges of the seam left on the *right* side. Naturally you don't want to wear anything with the seams on the outside, so you will have to turn the material wrong side out and make another seam to cover the raw edges. Look at the diagrams below.

Diagram A shows the first seam with the raw edges on the outside. Diagram B shows the second seam which covers up the raw edges and puts the seam inside where it belongs. That is a French seam.

Lay your two blouse pieces together with wrong sides facing each other. Make a ¼-inch seam on each shoulder. Turn the blouse wrong side out and make new shoulder seams to cover up the raw edges of the first ones.

Diagram A

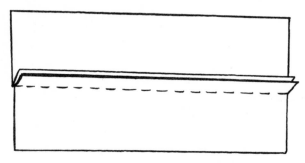

Make a ¼-inch seam on the right side of the garment as the first step in making a French seam.

Diagram B

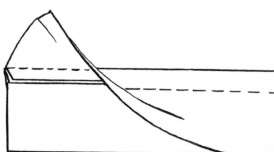

Turn the garment wrong side out and make another seam to cover the raw edges of the first seam.

After you have joined both shoulders, you are ready to hem the sleeve extensions. Baste a narrow hem from one notch to the other. Stitch it on the machine or by hand. Before you hem the sleeve extension, look at the diagram and the photograph which show you how to hem.

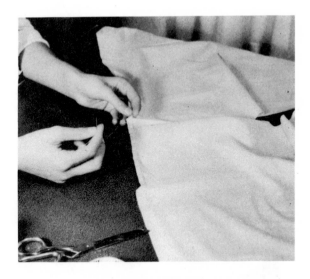

A hem is made by folding the raw edge twice so it is hidden and then stitching this fold.

After the sleeve extensions have been hemmed, you will be ready to French seam the sides of the blouse. Lay the blouse right side out with the back and front notches together. Baste the sides together from the underarm notch to the bottom edge. Do this on both sides. Machine stitch ¼ inch from the edge. Pull out the basting, and turn the blouse wrong side out. Now seam the sides again to finish the French seams. Baste and then stitch. Pull out the bastings. Make a narrow hem at the bottom edge of the blouse.

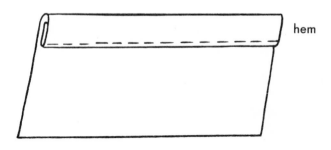

hem

Baste the sleeve hems before you machine stitch them. Make the hems ¼ inch wide.

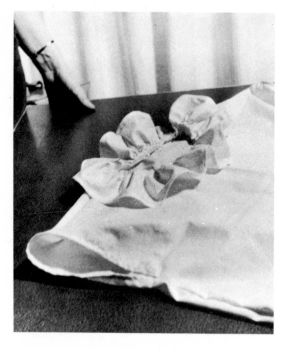

Now you are ready to finish the neckline of the blouse. The first thing to do is to bind the *selvedge* side of your ruffle. Machine stitch the white bias tape to this edge. Gather the cut edge of the ruffle until it measures about ½ inch larger than the neck opening. Make a French seam to join the two ends.

Pin the finished ruffle to the neckline of the blouse. Have the seam at the center of the back. Machine stitch the ruffle to the blouse. Make a narrow seam. After it is stitched trim off the raw edge so that the seam is no wider than ¼ inch all the way around.

Finish the neckline by covering the raw edge with a strip of bias tape. Start the binding at the center of the back. Baste the binding and be sure to cover all the raw edges. When you get back to where you started, leave about ½ inch of tape to turn under. You had better catch this end with a few hand stitches.

Machine stitch the binding and then remove the basting threads.

The tool this girl is using is just as important to good sewing as a sewing machine. When you sew, have the iron and ironing board where you can use them easily and often!

Sewing Dictionary

Basting Basting is a long running stitch that is used to hold two pieces of material together until they are sewed permanently.

Bias The diagonal grain of the cloth. Cloth that is cut on the bias is cut kitty-corner.

Binding A narrow piece of bias-cut material is used to finish an edge of cloth.

Facing A piece of cloth cut to finish an edge such as a neckline, front or back opening, or sleeve. The facing is usually sewed to the outside of the garment and then turned in so that it won't show. It finishes the edge neatly.

Fray Threads pulling out from a cut edge of cloth. A frayed edge is ragged with loose threads.

French seam A narrow seam that is sewed first on the right side of the garment and then turned and sewed on the inside in order to cover all the ragged edges. Usually made on lightweight material.

Gather To gather is to pull togther into little folds. This is done with a small running stitch by hand or with the gathering foot on the machine.

Hem To hem is to fold up the edge of the cloth twice so that the ragged edge is covered, and then the fold is sewed down.

Notch A notch is a cut in the edge of the pattern to show where to join other pattern pieces or to indicate distance.

Pink To cut an edge of cloth into little zigzags so the edges will not fray.

Placket The opening in a dress or skirt that makes it easy to get into.

Pleat A fold in a piece of cloth.

Raveling The threads of material beginnning to come apart into separate threads.

Seam A seam is the line of stitching that joins two pieces of cloth together.

Selvedge The woven edge of the cloth that is finished to prevent raveling.

Tack To tack is to stitch two pieces of cloth together lightly.